CURRICULUM AND EVALUATION

S T A N D A R D S

FOR SCHOOL MATHEMATICS

ADDENDA SERIES, GRADES K–6

F I F T H - G R A D E   B O O K

Grace Burton

Douglas Clements

Terrence Coburn

John Del Grande

John Firkins

Jeane Joyner

Miriam A. Leiva

Mary M. Lindquist

Lorna Morrow

Miriam A. Leiva, Series Editor

NATIONAL COUNCIL OF
TEACHERS OF MATHEMATICS

Copyright © 1992 by
THE NATIONAL COUNCIL OF TEACHERS OF MATHEMATICS, INC.
1906 Association Drive, Reston, Virginia 22091-1593
All rights reserved

Third printing 1993

Library of Congress Cataloging-in-Publication Data:

Fifth-grade book / Grace Burton ... [et al.].
        p.   cm. — (Curriculum and evaluation standards for school
    mathematics addenda series. Grades K–6)
      Includes bibliographical references.
      ISBN 0-87353-315-1 (vol.). — ISBN 0-87353-309-7 (set)
      1. Mathematics—Study and teaching (Elementary)   I. Burton,
    Grace M.   II. National Council of Teachers of Mathematics.
    III. Series.
    QA135.5.F49   1992
    372.7—dc20   91-45680
                                                         QA   CIP
                                                         135.5
                                                         .F49
                                                         1992

Photographs are by Patricia Fisher; artwork is by Lynn Gohman and Don Christian.

Printed in the United States of America

FOREWORD

The *Curriculum and Evaluation Standards for School Mathematics* (NCTM 1989a) describes a framework for revising and strengthening school mathematics. This visionary document provides a set of guidelines for K–12 mathematics curricula and for evaluating both the mathematics curriculum and students' progress. It not only addresses what mathematics students should learn but also how they should learn it.

As the document was being developed, it became apparent that supporting publications would be needed to interpret and illustrate how the vision could be translated realistically into classroom practices. A Task Force on the Addenda to the Curriculum and Evaluation Standards for School Mathematics, chaired by Thomas Rowan and composed of Joan Duea, Christian Hirsch, Marie Jernigan, and Richard Lodholz, was appointed by Shirley Frye, then NCTM president. The Task Force's recommendations on the scope and nature of the supporting publications were submitted to the Educational Materials Committee, which subsequently framed the Addenda Project.

Central to the Addenda Project was the formation of three writing teams—consisting of classroom teachers, mathematics supervisors, and university mathematics educators—to prepare a series of publications, the Addenda Series, targeted at mathematics instruction in grades K–6, 5–8, and 9–12. The purpose of the series is to clarify and illustrate the message of the *Curriculum and Evaluation Standards*. The underlying themes of problem solving, reasoning, communication, and connections are woven throughout the materials, as is the view of assessment as a means of guiding instruction. Activities have been field tested by teachers to ensure that they reflect the realities of today's classrooms.

It is envisioned that the Addenda Series will be a source of ideas by teachers as they begin to implement the recommendations in the NCTM *Curriculum and Evaluation Standards*. Individual volumes in the series are appropriate for in-service programs and for preservice courses in teacher education programs.

A project of this magnitude required the efforts and talents of many people over an extended time. Sincerest appreciation is extended to the authors and the editor and to the following teachers who played key roles in developing, revising, and trying out the materials for the *Fifth-Grade Book:* Marcia E. Dana, Angela C. Gardner, Jan Luquirre, Cynthia S. Parker, and Deborah Shotwell. Finally, this project would not have materialized without the outstanding technical support supplied by Cynthia Rosso and the NCTM publications staff.

Bonnie H. Litwiller
Addenda Project Coordinator

PREFACE

Something exciting is happening in many elementary school classrooms! A vision of an innovative mathematics program is coming alive. There *is* a shift in emphasis in the teaching and learning of mathematics. Teachers are encouraging children to investigate, discuss, question, and verify. They are focusing on explorations and dialogues. They are using various strategies to assess students' progress. They are making mathematics accessible to all children while exposing them to the value and the beauty of mathematics. Teachers and students are excited, and their enthusiasm is contagious. You can *catch it* when you hear children confidently explaining their solutions to the class, when you see them modeling problems with manipulatives, and when you observe them using a variety of methods and materials to arrive at answers. Some children are working with paper and pencil or with calculators; others are sharpening their estimation and mental math skills. There is noise in these classrooms—the sounds of students actively participating in the class and constructing their own knowledge through experiences that will give them confidence in their own abilities and make them mathematically powerful.

> I remember my own experiences in mathematics in elementary school. The classroom was quiet; all you could hear was the movement of pencils across sheets of paper and an occasional comment from the teacher. I was often bored; work was done in silent isolation, rules were memorized, and many routine problems were worked using rules few of us understood. Mathematics didn't always make sense. It was something that you did in school, mostly with numbers, and that you didn't need outside the classroom.
>
> "Why are we doing this?" my friend whispered.
>
> "Because it's in the book," I replied.
>
> "Do it this way," the teacher would explain while writing another problem on the chalkboard. "When you finish, work the next ten problems in the book."

We must go beyond how we were taught and teach how we wish we had been taught. We must bring to life a vision of what a mathematics classroom should be.

Rationale for Change

These are challenging times for you, the teachers of elementary school mathematics, and for your students. Major reforms in school mathematics are advocated in reports that call for changes in the curriculum, in student and program evaluations, in instruction, and in the classroom environment. These reforms are prompted by the changing needs of our society, which demand that all students become mathematically literate to function effectively in a technological world. A richer mathematics program is also supported by an explosion of new mathematical knowledge—more mathematics has been created in this century than in all our previous history. Research studies on teaching and learning, with emphasis on *how children learn mathematics,* have had a significant impact on current practices and strengthen the case for reform. Advances in technology also dictate changes in content and teaching.

Our students, the citizens of tomorrow, need to learn not only *more* mathematics but also mathematics that is broader in scope. They must have a strong academic foundation to enable them to expand their knowledge, to interpret information, to make reasonable decisions, and to solve increasingly complex problems using various approaches and tools, including calculators and computers. Mathematics instruction must reflect and implement these revised educational goals and increased expectations.

The blueprint for reform is the *Curriculum and Evaluation Standards for School Mathematics* (National Council of Teachers of Mathematics 1989a), which identifies a set of standards for the mathematics curriculum in grades K–12 as well as standards for evaluating the quality of programs and students' performance. The *Curriculum and Evaluation Standards* sets forth a bold vision of what mathematics education in grades K–12 should be and describes how mathematics classrooms can fit the vision.

Mathematics as Sense Making

In the past, mathematics classrooms were dominated by instruction and performance of rote procedures "to get the right answer." The *Curriculum and Evaluation Standards* supports the view of school mathematics as a sense-making experience encompassing a wide range of content, instructional approaches, and evaluation techniques.

Four standards are closely woven into content and instruction: mathematics as problem solving, mathematics as communication, mathematics as reasoning, and mathematical connections. These strands are common themes that support all other standards throughout all grade levels.

A primary goal for the study of mathematics is to give children experiences that promote the ability *to solve problems* and that build mathematics from situations generated within the context of everyday experiences. Students are also expected *to make conjectures and conclusions* and *to discuss their reasoning* in words, both written and spoken; with pictures, graphs, and charts; and with manipulatives. Moreover, students learn *to value mathematics* when they *make connections* between topics in mathematics, between the concrete and the abstract, between concepts and skills, and between mathematics and other areas in the curriculum.

The Changing Roles of Students

Previous efforts to reform school mathematics focused primarily on the curriculum; the *Curriculum and Evaluation Standards* also deals with other factors—in particular, students—that affect and are affected by reforms. The role of students is redirected from passive recipients to active participants, from isolated workers to team members, from listeners to investigators and reporters, and from timid followers to intrepid explorers and risk takers. They are asked to develop, discuss, create, model, validate, and investigate to learn mathematics.

Many people, including students, believe that mathematics is for the privileged few. It is time to dispel that myth. All children, regardless of sex, socioeconomic background, language, race, or ethnic origin, can and must succeed in school mathematics. With proper instruction, encouragement, and high expectations, *all* students can do mathematics.

Your Role in Implementing the Standards

All elementary school teachers are teachers of mathematics. Thus, your role is to build your students' self-confidence and nurture their natural curiosity; to challenge them with rich problems through which they will learn to value mathematics and appreciate the order and beauty of mathematics; to provide them with a strong foundation for further study; and to encourage their mathematical ability and power.

The elementary school years are crucial in a child's cognitive and affective development, and you are the central figure. You structure class-

Did you know that there are almost a billion blades of grass in the school lawn? We counted, measured, and estimated to find out.

Math is like a language. It has numbers, figures, and symbols that mean something if you understand the language. We use blocks and pictures to help us learn math.

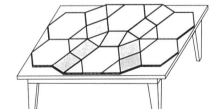
room experiences to implement the curriculum and create a supportive environment for learning to take place. In most activities you are the guide, the coach, the facilitator, and the instigator of mathematical explorations.

♦ You give children the gift of self-confidence. Through your careful grouping, astute questions, appropriate tasks, and realistic expectations, each student can experience success.

♦ Long after they forget childhood events, your students will remember you. Your excitement and interest permeate the room and stimulate their appreciation for mathematics.

♦ Through your classroom practices, you promote mathematical thinking, reasoning, and understanding.

♦ You lay the foundation on which further study will take place. You give students multiple strategies and tools to solve problems. The questions you ask and the problems you pose can capture your students' imagination, arouse their curiosity, and encourage their creativity.

♦ You facilitate the building of their knowledge by giving them interesting problems to solve, which leads to the development of concepts and important mathematical ideas.

♦ Rules, algorithms, and formulas emerge from student explorations guided by you, the teacher of mathematics.

Instructional Tools and the Standards

In order to implement the curriculum envisioned in the *Curriculum and Evaluation Standards,* we must carefully select and creatively use instructional tools. The textbook is only one of many important teaching resources. Children's development of concepts is fostered by their extensive use of physical materials to represent and describe mathematical ideas.

Calculators and computers are essential instructional tools at all levels. Through the appropriate use of these tools, students are able to solve realistic problems, investigate patterns, explore procedures, and focus on the steps to solve problems instead of on tedious computations.

Implementing the Evaluation Standards

Evaluation must be an integral part of teaching. A primary component of instruction is an ongoing assessment of what goes on in our classrooms. This information helps us make decisions about what we teach and how we teach it, about students' progress and feelings, and about our mathematics program.

The *Curriculum and Evaluation Standards* advocates many changes in curriculum, in instruction, and in the roles of students and teachers. None of these changes are more important than those related to evaluation. We must learn to use a variety of assessment instruments and not depend on pencil-and-paper tests alone. Tools such as observations, interviews, projects, reports, portfolios, diaries, and tests provide a more complete picture of what children understand and are able to use. Knowing what questions to ask is a skill we must develop.

When we test, we send a message about what we think is important. Because we encourage reasoning and communicating mathematically, we practice these skills. Because manipulatives and calculators are valuable tools for learning, we promote their use in the classroom. Because we want children to experience cooperative problem solving, we provide opportunities for group activities. *Not only must we evaluate what we want children to learn, but also how we want them to learn it.*

You and This Book

This booklet is part of the Curriculum and Evaluation for School Mathematics Addenda Series, Grades K–6. This series was designed to illustrate the standards and to help you translate them into classroom practice through—

♦ sample lessons and discussions that focus on the development of concepts;

♦ activities that connect models and manipulatives with concepts and with mathematical representations;

♦ problems that exemplify the use and integration of technology;

♦ teaching strategies that promote students' reasoning;

♦ approaches to evaluate students' progress;

♦ techniques to improve instruction.

In this booklet, both traditional and new topics are explored in four areas: Patterns, Number Sense and Operations, Making Sense of Data, and Geometry and Spatial Sense.

You will find classic fifth-grade activities that have been infused with an investigative flavor. These experiences include investigating tessellations and similarity with manipulatives and with the computer; setting the foundation for algebra by introducing the concept of variables with manipulatives and pictures; studying patterns to determine the rule for the *n*th term in a sequence of arrangements; conducting experiments in measurement and estimation with large numbers; extending estimation and computation activities to include decimals; making decisions by interpreting data gathered by students; introducing the concepts of randomness and sampling through experiments that are of interest to the class; and making connections to history and the study of other cultures through the use of patterns. You will also encounter a variety of problems and questions to explore with your fifth graders.

Change is an ongoing process that takes time and courage. It is not easy to go beyond comfort and security to try new things. As you use this book, pick and choose at will, and sample alternative approaches and ideas for instruction and assessment. Savor the freedom of change. All the documents in the world will not effect change in the classrooms; *only you can.*

The Challenge and the Vision

"I wonder why…?"

"What would happen if…?"   "Tell me about your pattern."

"Can you do it another way?"   "Our group has a different solution."

These inviting words give students the freedom to be creative, the confidence to solve problems, and the power to do mathematics. When you give your students the opportunity to construct their own knowledge, you are opening the doors of mathematics to *all* young learners.

This is the challenge. This is the vision.

Miriam A. Leiva, Editor
K–6 Addenda Series

5th Grade Survey

Sample: 15 students out of 93
Question: Hours of sleep each day
Range: 7 to 10 hours
Mode: 9 hours

Mrs. Frye showed us designs made by Native Americans and we learned how patterns help historians, archaeologists, and anthropologists study groups of people.

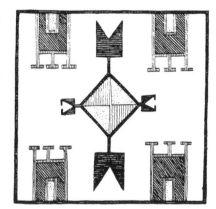

BIBLIOGRAPHY

National Council of Teachers of Mathematics. *Curriculum and Evaluation Standards for School Mathematics Addenda Series, Grades K–6,* edited by Miriam A. Leiva. Reston, Va.: The Council, 1991.

_____. *Curriculum and Evaluation Standards for School Mathematics Addenda Series, Grades 5–8,* edited by Frances R. Curcio. Reston, Va.: The Council, 1991.

_____. *Curriculum and Evaluation Standards for School Mathematics Addenda Series, Grades 9–12,* edited by Christian R. Hirsch. Reston, Va.: The Council, 1991.

_____. *Curriculum and Evaluation Standards for School Mathematics.* Reston, Va.: The Council, 1989a.

_____. *New Directions for Elementary School Mathematics.* 1989 Yearbook of the National Council of Teachers of Mathematics. Edited by Paul Trafton. Reston, Va.: The Council, 1989b.

_____. *Professional Standards for Teaching Mathematics.* Reston, Va.: The Council, 1991.

National Research Council. *Everybody Counts: A Report to the Nation on the Future of Mathematics Education.* Washington, D.C.: National Academy Press, 1989.

ACKNOWLEDGMENTS

At a time when the mathematics community was looking for directions on implementing the *Curriculum and Evaluation Standards for School Mathematics,* a group of dedicated professionals agreed to serve on the NCTM Elementary Addenda Project.

The task of editing and writing for this series has been challenging and rewarding. Selecting, testing, writing, and editing, as we attempted to translate the message of the *Standards* into classroom practices, proved to be a monumental and ambitious task. It could not have been done without the dedication and hard work of the authors, the teachers who reviewed and field tested the activities, and the editorial team.

My appreciation is extended to the main authors for each topic:

Grace Burton	Number Sense and Operations
Terrence Coburn	Patterns
John Del Grande and Lorna Morrow	Geometry and Spatial Sense
Mary M. Lindquist	Making Sense of Data

Our colleagues in the classrooms, Marcia E. Dana, Angela Gardner, Jan Luquirre, Cynthia Parker, and Deborah Shotwell, are thanked for giving us the unique perspective of teachers and children.

A special note of gratitude is owed to the individuals who served both as writers and as the editorial panel: Douglas Clements, John Firkins, and Jeane Joyner.

The editor also gratefully acknowledges the strong support of Bonnie Litwiller, Coordinator of the Addenda Project, and the assistance of Cynthia Rosso and the NCTM production staff for their guidance and help through the process of planning and producing this series of books.

The greatest reward for all who have contributed to this effort will be the knowledge that the ideas presented here have been implemented in elementary school classrooms, that these ideas have made realities out of visions, and that they have fostered improved mathematics programs for all children.

Miriam A. Leiva

PATTERNS

Fifth grade is a transition year between elementary school and middle school. Earlier work with patterns has enriched each student's basic understanding of mathematics. Investigating additional patterns develops and refines their mathematical abilities and enables them to describe, extend, create, analyze, and predict knowledgeably. The work with patterns in grade 5 shifts emphasis to general patterns, variables, and functions.

One activity in this section asks students to use patterns to construct figures and analyze the data in a table. The relationship shown between the term and the corresponding "trinumber" will be familiar to students—it is a multiplication table. Extensions of this activity encourage students to explore other tables by using quadrinumbers, pentinumbers, and other special numeric/geometric configurations. Another activity helps students visualize a variable.

Examining various patterns from the multicultural world in which we live helps children make mathematical connections. These connections enrich our lives and are bridges from the classroom to the outside world. Many cultures have developed repetitive patterns as decorations for their distinctive art forms: rugs, lace, jewelry, cloth, pottery, drums, and buildings. Each artifact can be analyzed and sorted by the type of transformation the design exhibits.

Additional connections can be made by having students do some library work. For example, researching African Kuba drum designs or strip patterns from Pueblo Indian pottery and reporting back to the class add another dimension to mathematical inquiry.

In the upper elementary grades, students need to broaden their pattern recognition abilities. These include analyzing, generalizing, and expressing more sophisticated patterns in numerical form. Recognizing these relationships provides a foundation for understanding more abstract algebraic concepts developed later.

Exploring patterns helps students develop mathematical power and instills in them an appreciation for the beauty of mathematics. (NCTM 1989a, p. 98)

Flips or Reflections

Slides or Translations

Turns or Rotations

PATTERNS AROUND US

Get ready. The purpose of this activity is to have students recognize and create designs by using reflections, translations, and rotations. These transformations are sometimes called *flips, slides,* and *turns.*

Collect fabric, wallpaper, and wrapping paper samples for the class to explore for flip, turn, and slide patterns. Give the students crayons, colored pens, paper strips, tracing or tissue paper, rubber stamps, and grid paper.

Get going. Discuss wallpaper designs, particularly the narrow border strips. Many wallpaper, fabric, and carpet designs feature symmetrical patterns.

Ask the students to use their art supplies to create a border design for their classroom similar to the narrow wallpaper border strips. Have them draw a simple figure that will be the unit, or *repetend,* of the strip design. To help them produce intricate designs, have them make a template of their unit figure on a small piece of tracing or tissue paper or acetate. Let them choose one or more of the transformations to create their own pattern strip. Have them flip, turn, or slide the template on the paper strip to make their border design.

After the students make such designs, encourage a discussion of the transformations used.

Ryan, tell me about your design.

What part of Sue's design is constantly repeating?

Who used slides in their designs?

If Meg had used a turn instead of a slide, what would her design have looked like?

Did anyone use two different transformations to form a design?

If I covered part of Andrea's design, could you tell me what I covered?

What would come next in Harry's design?

To explore transformations further, have the students draw the same design on four pieces of square paper. Let them experiment with ways to combine their congruent designs through a variety of transformations. For example, if the basic design is ◣, these are some of the possible combinations:

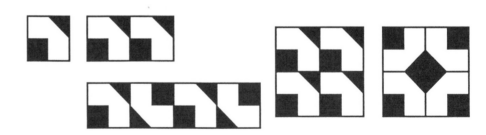

This activity can be extended in two dimensions as the students create wallpaper or tilelike patterns on their grid paper. Suggest they combine transformations to make their designs.

◆　　◆　　◆　　◆　　◆　　◆　　◆　　◆

Keep going. Every culture decorates its surroundings with patterns and designs. Ask the students to find patterns that are part of their family history or culture. Items that might be displayed could include Ukrainian eggs, American quilts, African drums, Navaho sand paintings, Spanish tiles, Scottish tartans, or any other item associated with a class member's heritage.

Tell the students that archaeologists excavate sites to learn about ethnic groups and tribes as cultural units. They use analytical techniques to determine if a tribal group is consistent in structuring its designs. If consistency is present, they are able to conclude that a whole group of sites represents the same culture.

Anthropologists use similar techniques to link populations across geographical boundaries and historical times.

Have the students choose a country or a culture, research the use of specific patterns in that culture, and make a report to the class. Suggest they use examples from music, art, and fabrics to illustrate their report. These reports will catch the eye of classroom visitors.

TRINUMBERS

Get ready. The purpose of this activity is to have children find a general rule for a pattern. The pattern used here relates a trinumber to its term in the sequence.

Students will need counters such as lima beans or tiles, paper, and pencils. Working in small groups will facilitate student explorations and discussions.

Get going. Give each group seventy to eighty counters. On the overhead projector or chalkboard, show the first three trinumbers.

How are these figures alike?

How are they different?

Is there a pattern? Tell me about it.

What will the next figure in the pattern look like?

How many counters are there in each figure?

Make a table to show how many counters it takes to make each figure. These are called trinumbers.

Allow the students time to construct and record the first seven trinumbers. Guide the students in looking at the difference between consecutive trinumbers.

Is it reasonable for 3 to be the constant difference? Why? Could 62 be a trinumber? How do you know?

Challenge the students to create a written description of the pattern that relates the term to the trinumber. Students will vary in the way they describe the pattern:

"The trinumbers are multiples of 3."

"Each trinumber is 3 more than the previous one."

"Multiply the term number by 3."

"Each new triangle needs 3 more counters."

Trinumbers

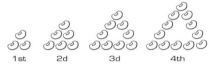

1st　　2d　　3d　　4th

Term	Trinumber
1	3
2	6
3	9
4	?
5	?

Each trinumber is found by counting the number of counters used to make its figure.

Terry and Jessica described the third trinumber this way:

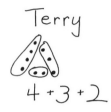

Terry

4 + 3 + 2

Jessica

3 times the dots on one side minus 3

Notice that the rule or the generalization comes from examining the table, but the models created with the counters and the pictures of the trinumbers give meaning to the table. Students who are visual learners need concrete and pictorial experiences to make connections and to build relationships.

When students build models of the terms and then record the results in a table, they are moving from learning about patterns to learning to use patterns. They need to be encouraged to examine the table both vertically and horizontally in trying to discover the rule in the nth number.

"Each side gets 1 more counter, and there are 3 sides."

The level of students' responses is a measure of the development of their mathematical power. Students who recognize and are able to describe patterns and relationships in more than one way are more likely to use patterns as a problem-solving strategy.

Ask the students if they can use their general rule to predict the tenth trinumber. Allow them time to verify their answer by drawing or building the tenth trinumber, if necessary.

Some students may be able to write the rule or the formula for the trinumbers: The expression $3n$ tells the relationship between the nth term and the nth trinumber. The answer for the fiftieth trinumber is 3×50, or 150. *What would the hundredth trinumber be?*

Ask the students to describe the relationship between the number of counters on each side of the triangle and the trinumber.

Keep going. Repeat this activity with quadrinumbers, pentinumbers, and hexinumbers. *How are these special numbers related to the multiplication tables?* Have the students write in their mathematics logs or to a friend, explaining what a quadrinumber is, what a pentinumber is, and what the general pentinumber and hexinumber rules are.

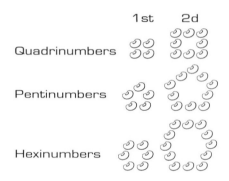

Define an "**L** number" as the number of dots needed to build an **L** shape in which the vertical and horizontal segments have an equal number of dots.

*Make the smallest **L** number. How many dots does it have?*

*What is the fifth **L** number? What is the sixth **L** number?*

Ask the students to make a table relating the term (first, second, third, …) and the corresponding **L** number. Have them describe the pattern. Some children may be able to write a mathematical expression that gives the nth **L** number, $2n + 1$.

Term	L Number
1	3
2	5
3	7
4	9
5	11
6	?

Have the students investigate other letter patterns. What would the first four **T** numbers be? The first three **S** numbers? The first five **M** numbers? Did all students have the same answers? Have the students explain their thinking to one another. This activity has implications for similarity—a topic explored in the chapter on geometry and spatial sense (p. 24).

Language—talking and writing about the models and the tables—is a bridge that helps students make connections.

NUMBER MAGIC

Get ready. The purpose of this activity is to have students investigate patterns involving arithmetic operations that can be generalized to a mathematical expression with a variable or a placeholder. Using calculators will allow students to experiment with a variety of examples as they search for patterns.

These activities review the meanings of whole number operations while preparing students for algebra.

Get going. Give the following sequence of steps to your students:

1. Choose any number.

2. Multiply your number by 6.

3. Add 12 to the result.

4. Take half.

5. Subtract 6.

6. Divide by 3.

7. Write your answer.

Have them work through the list of directions with different *chosen* numbers.

Examples:　1. Choose 10　　　　　　　　1. Choose 15

　　　　　　2. 6 × 10 = 60　　　　　　　2. 6 × 15 = 90

　　　　　　3. 60 + 12 = 72　　　　　　3. 90 + 12 = 102

　　　　　　4. 72 ÷ 2 = 36　　　　　　4. 102 ÷ 2 = 51

　　　　　　5. 36 – 6 = 30　　　　　　5. 51 – 6 = 45

　　　　　　6. 30 ÷ 3 = 10　　　　　　6. 45 ÷ 3 = 15

Challenge the students to explain why they always seem to end with the same number with which they started. Allow time for them to discuss this with their neighbors and to offer possible reasons. Then suggest that they can solve the puzzle, "Why do we always end up with the *chosen* number," by thinking of the original number as a "box of raisins." Guide them in verbalizing each step in the directions and help them to recognize that the number of raisins in the box is not as important as what happens (the process) to the box.

You will find it helpful to use concrete objects—actual boxes and raisins—to illustrate the steps. The box serves as a *placeholder*, or *variable*, for the chosen number.

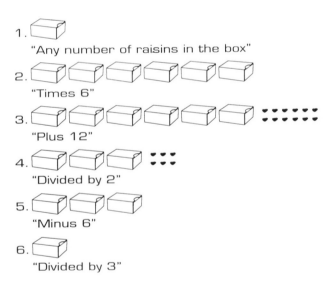

Note: the process is summarized by $\left[\left(\dfrac{6\,\boxed{} + 12}{2}\right) - 6\right] \div 3$.

Guide the students in seeing that each arithmetic operation done to their original number (the box) was undone in some successive step.

Keep going. Explore other number magic puzzles with the students. Encourage them to work with a partner to write the rules for the processes pictured and to be prepared to explain them.

Ask the students to write a set of rules corresponding to the following picture:

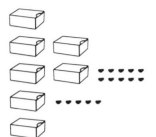

Answer:

1. Choose a number.

2. Double it, or multiply by 2.

3. Add 10.

4. Divide by 2, or take half.

5. Subtract 5.

$$\text{or} \quad \left(\dfrac{2\,\boxed{} + 10}{2}\right) - 5$$

You can also make up puzzles that will always result in the same answer, regardless of the chosen number. For example, ask the students to choose a number, triple it, add 6, divide by 3, and subtract the original number. What is the result?

1. Choose a number.

2. Triple it.

3. Add 6.

4. Divide by 3.

5. Subtract the original number.

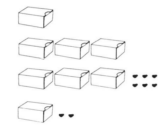

$$\text{or} \quad \left(\dfrac{3\,\boxed{} + 6}{3}\right) - \boxed{}$$

Did everyone get the same answer? Why?

Have partners or pairs of students design their own sets of directions that result in a preselected number. After they check both their written and their "pictured" directions, have them switch with other groups.

Collect the student-generated puzzles into a book. Sharing the book with other fourth, fifth, and sixth graders would be fun for the class.

NUMBER SENSE AND OPERATIONS

As they learn new ideas or solve new problems, students enrich their own thought processes and skills by drawing on previously developed ideas; this ability to integrate ideas and concepts fosters students' confidence in their own thinking as well as in their skills of communication. (NCTM 1989a, p. 85)

Children with number sense use numbers flexibly and choose the most appropriate representation of a number for a given circumstance. When solving problems, they are able to select from various strategies and tools—they know when to estimate, when to use paper and pencil, and when to use a calculator. They predict with some accuracy the result of an operation and describe the relationships between various forms of numbers. This "friendliness with numbers" goes far beyond mere memorization of algorithms and number facts and implies an ability to recognize when operations are required and when they have been correctly performed.

Students with number sense typically use their skills appropriately in a variety of settings inside and outside the classroom. Both on tests and in real-world situations, fifth graders model and use numbers in many ways to assess the results of their mathematical reasoning.

Active fifth graders enjoy working together to investigate puzzling events and to solve mysteries. Activities presented here try to capitalize on students' curiosity by motivating them to explore mathematical questions and to make and verify predictions.

To provide students with a lasting sense of number and number relationships, learning should be grounded in experience related to aspects of everyday life or to the use of concrete materials designed to reflect underlying mathematical ideas. (NCTM 1989a, p. 87)

FIND THE MISSING LINK

Opportunities to explain, conjecture, and defend one's ideas orally and in writing can stimulate deeper understandings of concepts and principles. (NCTM 1989a, p. 78)

Get ready. The purpose of this activity is to have students practice estimating and computing with decimals. Being able to place the correct number in the link requires facility with both estimation and computation. Determining the missing link provides a bridge from arithmetic to algebra. Calculator use is an integral part of this activity.

Draw chains, such as the one shown, on an overhead transparency. Write decimal numbers in the first four links.

Get going. For each problem, ask the students to look at the chain, estimate the answer, and explain how they arrived at the estimate. For the problem above, a student said that she estimated by rounding to 20 + 10 - 10 + 8, or 28. Another student explained that the difference between 13.4 and 12.5 is about 1; his estimate was 20 + 1 + 8, or 29. Pose questions to the class to encourage a variety of estimation strategies and to reinforce computational skills.

Will the answer be more that 20? More than 30? How do you know?

Will the order in which you do the calculations make a difference?

Suppose we add 10 to each number in the problem. How would that affect the result?

Allow ample time for class discussion. Calculators can be used throughout the activity to determine good estimates and to compute answers. Do several examples of the same type before proceeding to more challenging problems.

Display another chain, such as the one below. Pose questions and accept suggestions from the class as you work together to estimate and solve the problem.

Is this one harder to solve? Why?

Explore other links with the class. Encourage further class discussion.

Is more than one answer possible?

What is the smallest number that you think can be put in the first link?

What is the largest number that you feel can be put in the next open link?

Challenge the class with problems with missing operations, such as the one below.

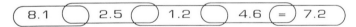

If addition, subtraction, and multiplication were used to form the above chain, what other answers are possible?

Discuss any variations that may be suggested and include the use of whole numbers and fractions in the missing link problems.

Keep going. Put the students in small groups and have them generate their own missing link problems. Suggest that each student group keep answer keys for their problems. Ask them to exchange their problems with other groups.

SKATING OFF THE SNACK

Get ready. The purpose of this activity is to have students generate and solve problems with real-world data. Put students in groups of three or four and give each group a copy of Skating Off the Snack (p. 15) and a calculator. You may wish to make an overhead transparency to use during the lesson.

When students find the numeric value of a missing link, they are, in fact, solving an algebraic equation where the empty link takes the place of the variable, x.

Student responses:

Merrie: *"I subtracted 3 from 6 and then added 5. I got 8, so I had to subtract 2 to get 6 on the right-hand side."*

Ralph: *"I added 6 and 5 and got 11. I subtracted 3 and got 8, which was 2 more than 6. So I put 2 in the empty link."*

Some types of link problems:

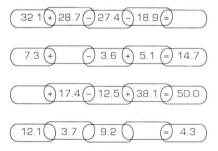

This activity introduces students to the health concepts that calories taken in provide energy for the body and that each type of food has a caloric value. The study of calories and energy relates this mathematical lesson to physics, biology, and chemistry.

Get going. Allow time for the students to read and discuss the material before proceeding. Pose and answer questions to help the students focus on the activity.

How many calories per minute will Pat burn up? How did you get that?

Will Jerry use more or fewer calories per minute than Pat? Why? Who will use the fewest? How did you decide that?

Whose lunch had the most calories? What could Pat have for lunch that could be skated off in about half an hour?

Can you select a lunch that would be about 1000 calories?

When the students are familiar with the data, suggest that they write other problems. When they have done so, assign the children to groups of four and suggest that they exchange papers with another group and attempt to solve the new problems.

How many more calories in Li's lunch than Jerry's?

Pat ways less than Li. Who has to skate longer to use up the same number of calories?

What lunch would equal 1,200 calories?

How many calories in a BLT?

If Pat and Li were on one side of a seesaw and Lou and Jerry were on the other, which side would go down?

Lead class discussions about weight, mass, and gravity. If a kilogram scale is available, have the students weigh themselves, decide on a menu, and compute how long they would need to skate to burn off the calories in their snack.

Keep going. The activity is easily extended by using other lunch selections and sports or by varying the weights. Have the students consult a variety of sources to find out the number of calories used in various physical activities. Cookbooks are a resource for calorie charts.

Ask the groups to pose additional problems, discuss solution strategies, solve the problems, and write them on file cards. Collect the cards and share them with another classroom. You might contact a teacher in another school and have the students exchange the problems with that teacher's class by mail or a computer network.

HOW MANY BLADES OF GRASS ARE THERE?

Get ready. The purpose of this activity is to show students that sampling, measuring, averaging, and rounding add to a person's understanding of the large numbers used in the world around us.

Many children and adults have no idea how much a million is, let alone a billion. This activity helps give meaning to such outlandishly large numbers.

You will need a small sampling square for each student. Have the students make their squares by cutting a hole 1 centimeter on a side from the center of a 3" x 5" file card. A trundle wheel or a measuring tape is also needed for this activity.

Get going. Explain to the class that they will collect information to help them estimate how many blades of grass there are in the school lawn or field. Send the students outdoors to count the number of blades of grass that can be seen through the hole in their index card when the card is placed on the lawn.

Questions are apt to arise: "Should we count the dead grass?" and "What's a blade?" Have each student report the number of blades of grass found.

Assign two students to measure the dimensions of the lawn by using the trundle wheel or the measuring tape. Round the lawn's dimensions to the nearest meter, then find its area.

Situations that allow students to experience problems with "messy" numbers or too much or not enough information or that have multiple solutions, each with different consequences, will better prepare them to solve problems they are likely to encounter in their daily lives. (NCTM 1989a, p. 76)

Number sense is knowing that an answer is "in the ballpark." Approximate solutions to complicated problems often suffice, especially if we are interested in the magnitude of the number, not an exact count.

A teacher in Washington reports that after several years of sampling on a lawn measuring 70 × 81 meters, students have never been able to show that more than 950 000 000 blades of grass were growing there. Students like to use this lawn as their billion dollar counter.

Challenge the class to figure out how to use the information they have gathered to find the total number of blades of grass. Discuss possible strategies. Provide ample time for the students to explain and justify the solution to the problem. Lead them to compute the number of centimeter squares needed to fill the lawn. Multiply the class average by the number of square centimeters needed to cover the lawn to get a good estimate of the number of blades of grass in the designated area.

In 1990 the national debt was over a trillion dollars. How many rooms the size of the classroom would be needed to store the national debt if it were paid in one-dollar bills?

Keep going. This activity can be linked to a social studies unit or to a current event heard on a national news broadcast. How large is the national debt? How large a lawn area would we need to have enough blades of grass to represent the national debt? How long would it take to mow a lawn of that size? How much would the clippings weigh? After discussing these and similar questions, the students will have a better understanding of large numbers.

The question of satisfactory sampling should be raised. (Refer to the chapter on data sense for additional sampling activities.) Did every blade have an equal opportunity to be counted? Probably not. If you send a group of students out to do this job, they usually bunch around each other and do not spread out over the lawn. This furnishes an excellent opportunity to talk about sampling errors. Should you count dead grass? What is a blade? These and similar questions provide a chance to clarify important concerns.

NUMBER DETECTIVE

If students are to become mathematically powerful, they must be flexible enough to approach situations in a variety of ways and recognize the relationships among different points of view. (NCTM 1989a, p. 84)

Get ready. The purpose of this activity is to have students use reasoning skills in a number line context. The activity involves the recognition of the relationships between numbers and can focus on whole numbers, fractions, or decimals as appropriate to your class.

Give each student a copy of the Number Detective worksheet and several long, narrow strips of paper. You may wish to make an overhead transparency of the worksheet.

Get going. Tell the students that they are detectives who must discover what number should be put in the boxes on each number line. Suggest that folding the paper strips may give them clues to what the number should be. Encourage them to use previously completed examples as they solve each new "mystery." When the students have finished, call on several of them to explain how they knew what number was indicated by the box. Encourage them to use proportional thinking as they explain their answers. (Example: The first box in the second line had to be 1/10 of 50 because 10 is 1/10 of 100.)

Keep going. Draw additional arrows and boxes on your transparency copy of the Number Detective. Select students to fill in the appropriate number and justify their decisions to the class.

Encourage the students to work in pairs; one student draws a line segment of any length, selects and labels the "endpoints," and indicates the placement of boxes; the other student fills in the missing numbers.

TARGET PRACTICE

Get ready. The purpose of this activity is to have students use mental arithmetic.

Prepare three number cubes with numbers on their faces as follows:

cube 1: 0, 1, 2, 3, 4, 5

cube 2: 6, 7, 8, 9, 1, 0

cube 3: 10, 10, 10, 1, 1, 1

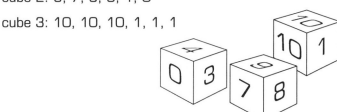

Feedback to students can have a variety of forms, including written or oral comments or numerical scores on a specific exercise. (NCTM 1989a, p. 209)

Get going. Have a student write down a number less than 100, toss the three cubes, and attempt to make an equation that results in the target number by using the three numbers showing "up" on the cubes. Allow any operations to be used. The student who comes closest to the target number wins.

Keep going. You may wish to use more cubes or to make some of the faces decimals or fractions.

Divide the class into teams. Throw the number cubes and record the results on the board. Class members have three minutes to write down as many mathematical sentences as they can, using these numbers. When time is called, team 1 reads their sentences. If anyone on team 2 has that sentence, both teams cross it off. Any sentence not crossed off (i.e., obtained by only one team) results in a point for that team. The first team to reach a designated score wins. For example, 2, 6, and 10 are recorded on the board. Here are just a few possible answers:

$2 + 6 + 10 = 18$

$2 \times 6 + 10 = 22$

$6 \div 2 + 10 = 13$

Students' mathematical dispositions are manifested in the way they approach tasks—whether with confidence, willingness to explore alternatives, perseverance, and interest—and in their tendency to reflect on their own thinking. (NCTM 1989a, p. 233)

A variation of Target Practice is the game Decade. Use a regular deck of playing cards, allowing the ace to be 1 and removing the face cards. Players choose a target decade (i.e., 20, 30, 40) between 10 and 100. Each player draws four cards and uses any operation to try to come closest to the target decade. A player must use all four numbers drawn. Players could work as a team and plan together.

Target decade is 30:

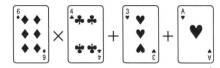

NUMBER DETECTIVE

Each number line segment has one or more arrows pointing to a specific spot on that number line. Below each arrow is a box. Write in the box the number that corresponds to the arrow's position on the number line.

● ↓ ↓ ●
0 [50] [ ] 100

● ↓ ↓ ●
0 [ ] [ ] 10

● ↓ ↓ ●
0 [ ] [ ] 1

● ↓ ↓ ●
100 [ ] [ ] 300

● ↓ ↓ ●
1 [ ] [ ] 3

● ↓ ↓ ●
0 [ ] [ ] 500

● ↓ ↓ ●
0 [ ] [ ] 50

● ↓ ↓ ●
0 [ ] [ ] 5

● ↓ ↓ ●
0 [ ] [ ] 0 5

Fact: Figure skating uses up about 1 calorie a minute for each 5 kilograms of body weight.

Skater	Weight	Lunch
Pat	50 kg	BLT (2 slices of bacon, 2 leaves of lettuce, 2 slices of tomato, mayo), banana
Lou	78 kg	2 hot dogs on rolls, apple
Jerry	40 kg	hamburger on a roll, orange, apple
Li	62 kg	hamburger on a roll, banana, slice of apple pie

Calorie Chart

Food	Amount	Calories
Broiled hamburger	4 oz.	180
Broiled hot dog	1	170
Roll	1	115
Bacon	2 slices	100
Lettuce	2 leaves	10
Tomato	1 slice	5
Bread	2 slices	140
Banana	1	100
Apple	1	100
Orange, large	1	95
Mayonnaise	1 T	110
Apple pie	1 slice	405

MAKING SENSE OF DATA

A knowledge of statistics is necessary if students are to become intelligent consumers who can make critical and informed decisions. (NCTM 1989a, p. 105)

Many people consider statistics an advanced topic of study not needed by fifth-grade students. Nothing could be further from the truth. Fifth graders can use many ideas associated with statistics to make sense of data. The activities in this section focus on sampling and randomness. Although these are sophisticated ideas, they are appropriate for fifth graders and need to be introduced early; the full development will occur over many years.

In making decisions, we often take samples of the whole population because it is impractical or too costly to collect all possible information. One type of sample is a random sample—each member of the population is equally likely to be chosen. The size of the sample is an important consideration that depends on many factors. In this set of activities, the idea that the size of the sample makes a difference is presented informally. There is plenty of time to refine such ideas later.

Students should talk about their ideas and use the results of their experiments to model situations or predict events. (NCTM 1989a, p. 109)

The following activities are described in detail. If you are comfortable with the ideas, modify, or let your students modify, the activities to answer questions that interest them. Remember that posing problems and clarifying questions are important steps in working with data.

MYSTERY CHARACTERS

Get ready. The purpose of this activity is to help students understand the meaning of a random sample and why random samples are used. In the next activity, they will use a random sample to make predictions.

Choose a mystery or another story with several strong characters. Suggested titles are *Wait till Helen Comes, The Westing Game, The Mystery of Drear House,* any title in the Encyclopedia Brown series, or any book by John Bellairs. Before beginning this activity, have the students read the mystery, or read it to the class. Each child will need a 3" × 5" card.

Students should have many opportunities to observe the interaction of mathematics with other school subjects.... (NCTM 1989a, p. 84)

Get going. Have the children imagine that *one* of three characters from the mystery is to be invited to their school to speak. Ask the students,

How will the class decide which character to invite?

Give the class several options, such as those below, and let them decide why each option would not be suitable:

♦ The teacher could decide.

♦ A committee of five boys (or five girls) could decide.

♦ The tallest student could decide.

♦ The students with straight A's could decide.

The students should recognize that none of these options is certain to represent the class fairly. They may suggest taking a vote, which would be a practical solution for this situation. Discuss with the students the problem of obtaining each person's opinion from a large group and why it is desirable to take a sample.

The samples suggested above are not random. In a random sample, each person must have an equal chance of being chosen. One way to get a random sample of the students is to place all their names in a box, shake the box well, and draw the sample.

Tell the students that they are going to investigate whether a random sample of their class can predict whom the class wants to invite. Have each student write his or her name on a 3" × 5" card, along with the name of the character the student wants to invite.

Take several random samples of five students by drawing five cards at one time. Return the names to the box after recording the results of each sample.

After each sample, ask the students if they can make a prediction about the entire class's choice. As soon as most students feel confident about what the class's choice will be, stop taking samples and check their predictions. If the presented evidence is not convincing, take larger samples, say of ten children. On the one hand, children should begin to get the feel that if the vote is really close, a small sample is probably not adequate to use for a prediction. On the other hand, if the results from several small samples are analyzed, there may be enough information to make a prediction.

Keep going. There are many experiments that require making a prediction about a whole population from a sample. For example, students may draw samples of 5, 10, or 20 chips from a box of 100 chips (50 red, 30 blue, and 20 yellow) to see if they can predict the proportions of colors of the 100 chips. Remember to replace each chip in the box after each draw.

Or you may want to simulate a fanciful, but possible, mysterious situation:

> A detective, Stella, is hired to select a town for Mr. Li. He wants to move to the most honest town he can find from the three towns whose populations are described below.
>
> Pennytown: 70 honest and 30 dishonest citizens
> Dimetown: 50 honest and 50 dishonest citizens
> Quartertown: 30 honest and 70 dishonest citizens
>
> But the descriptions are garbled and no one really knows which town goes with which description. Mr. Li pays Stella $100 to find out. Each mayor agrees to send Stella samples (random, of course) of five people. Being a stellar detective, Stella can tell which people are honest and which are not. The only catch is that each sample of five costs $5.00. Can Stella find out and still make money?

Have three bags of chips, each with 100 chips of two colors to represent the honest and dishonest citizens in the proportions given above. Label the bags A, B, and C. Assign the students to small discussion groups to plan a sampling strategy before they draw any samples. For example, one group may decide to draw ten samples of five chips each from A and B and none from C. Allow each group to implement their strategy and then write to Stella, advising her whether or not to accept $100 to complete this task.

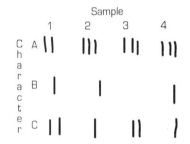

OUR AVERAGE DAY

In grades 5-8, the mathematics curriculum should include exploration of statistics in real-world situations so that students can systematically collect, organize, and describe data. (NCTM 1989a, p. 105)

One class decided it was better to talk to the students in each sample the day after the designated day. Thus the Tuesday group gathered their data before school on Wednesday.

Get ready. The purpose of this activity is to have students collect and analyze data that describe the average member of a population. The students design a questionnaire, choose a random sample to interview, and analyze and present the results.

Students should work in groups of about four. You will need seven groups, one for each day of the week. If you have a small class, you may want to restrict the days selected for the study.

No special materials are needed; however, if students have computers available, they could use graphing software to help them analyze and present their data.

Restrict your sample to under 100 fifth-grade students. You will need a list of all participating students.

Get going. Pose this question:

How do you think fifth-grade students in our school spend their time?

Lead a discussion about some possible activities and the number of students engaged in them.

Assign the students to groups and give each group the name of a day of the week. Have each group design a questionnaire for the assigned day. The questionnaires for Monday through Friday may be quite similar, and the ones for Saturday and Sunday may be very different from the weekday ones. Have each group try its questions and format as a pilot study with a few students from another group.

Let the class decide on a common questionnaire, using the best ideas from each group. Students may insist on two questionnaires, one reflecting weekday activities and the other reflecting weekend activities. Talk about why a questionnaire should be rather simple and short.

Prepare ten copies of the questionnaire for each group. Before they carry out their surveys, have them discuss how they plan to choose their sample of ten students. If they have done the previous activity, they should suggest taking a random sample.

Discuss with the students how they might take such a sample. Provide the list of all the students from which the sample will be taken. If the students' names are numbered, then the sample can be made by selecting numbers randomly.

There are several ways to generate random numbers:

Spinner. Spin for the ones digit and again for the tens digit.

Numbers 0 through 9 in a box. Draw for the ones digit, replace the card, and draw again for the tens digit.

Computer. Use a programming language such as Logo. To select a sample of size 10 from 87 students, type [REPEAT 10 [PRINT + RANDOM 87].

Random number table. Use a table of random numbers.

Let each group draw their random sample of ten numbers, find the names of the ten people, and apportion the interview task. When the group members have collected the information, they should try to organize it and write about what they have found. Remind the students to keep their original data; if the class has questions, they can return to the information. Here is the first page of one group's report.

There was a lively discussion in one class about why no TV was watched on Wednesday and why more time was spent eating on the week-end. The students were appalled that the students in one class reported that they spent no time on art or on science. The teacher handled this tactfully by helping the children to see they should not overgeneralize from one week to the entire year.

Students in grades 5-8 have a keen interest in trends in music, movies, fashion, and sports. (NCTM 1989a, p. 105)

Our Monday

From our sample of 10 students out of 87, we listed the range of hours. This didn't help us much. Our teacher told us about the mode. That's easy; it is the one that happens most.

Here's what we found.

	range	mode
sleeping	$8 - 10\frac{1}{2}$	9
eating	$\frac{1}{2} - 1\frac{1}{2}$	$1\frac{1}{2}$
School	$6\frac{1}{2}$	$6\frac{1}{2}$
math	1 to $1\frac{1}{2}$	1
science	0 to $\frac{1}{2}$	0
p.e.	0 to $\frac{1}{2}$	$\frac{1}{2}$
l.a.	$\frac{1}{2}$ to 1	1
reading	1	1
s.s.	0 to 1	$\frac{1}{2}$
health	$\frac{1}{2}$	$\frac{1}{2}$
art	0 to $\frac{1}{2}$	0
music	$\frac{1}{2}$	$\frac{1}{2}$
tv	$0 - 3$	$\frac{1}{2}$
reading	$0 - 2$	$1\frac{1}{2}$
fiddling around	$0 - 4$	3
homework	$0 - 2$	$\frac{1}{2}$
lessons (music)	$0 - 1$	0
other	$0 - 2$	2

We talked a lot about what this meant and how to present it to the others in our class.

When all the groups are finished, discuss their findings and see if the class can arrive at a composite description of a weekday of an average fifth-grade student in your school. For example, the average fifth-grade student spends seven hours at school and nine hours sleeping.

Keep going. Challenge your students to compare themselves to students in other fifth grades in your city or state. They could sample a class in another school by sending the questionnaire with a cover letter to explain the project.

The students could also choose other topics to survey: What does the average student like to eat, to read, to watch on TV? What hand do most students write with? What color eyes do most students have? What color hair? How many students can curl their tongue? What is their favorite song?

A RANDOM WALK

One teacher provided transparencies and markers to be used over the blackline master so that children could begin each walk with a clean grid. Others encouraged the students to use their pencils lightly.

Get ready. The purpose of this activity is to have students use a random number table to generate data. Students also will develop an intuitive notion about adding positive and negative numbers and some beginning ideas about probability.

Students should work in pairs, one reading the numbers from the random number table and the other making the steps on the number line. Each pair will need a copy of A Random Walk (p. 23).

Get going. Usually when we take a walk we know where we are going, but there are times when we just meander. A random walk, like the ones that the students will take in this activity, is determined by chance. Tell the students that they are going to investigate such a walk on a number line.

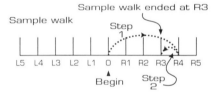

Each step of this walk is specified by a number (1 through 6) in a random number table. For each walk, a pair of students will choose six adjacent numbers in a row or a column, beginning at any place in the table. These six numbers specify the six steps; an even number will indicate a move to the right and an odd number will mean a move to the left. For example, if the first two numbers in the selected row were 4 and 1, the first step would be a move of 4 to the right from 0 and the second step would be a move of 1 to the left from the end of the first step. The final position would be R3.

◆   ◆   ◆   ◆   ◆   ◆   ◆   ◆

Make a transparency of A Random Walk and practice walking on the number line several times with the class before having the students collect the data from ten walks. When the students are comfortable moving on the number line, ask them what would happen if many random walks were taken on this section of the number line.

About how many times out of 100 will a walk end on this segment?

How many steps will most walks take before going off?

On which step will most walks go off the segment?

Is a walk more likely to go off at the right or at the left? Why?

Will more walks end to the left or to the right of 0?

After talking about these predictions with the students, let each pair take ten walks, recording where they land on the number line or recording which step during their walk ended off this portion of the number line. This information should be recorded in the "right off" or "left off" columns.

Discuss how the results of the student pairs compare to the predictions they made. Then, combine the data for the class and see how the combined data compare to the results.

Challenge the students to tell how the walk could end off this number line in 2 steps, in 3 steps, and in 4 steps. Many will see that the only way a walk could be off the number line in 2 steps is for the first two numbers to be 6s. There are several ways to go off in 3 steps and many more ways to go off in 4 steps.

If the class is interested, repeat the activity to see if the results are the same. They may enjoy generating the random numbers with number cubes (1–6) instead of using the random number table.

How would the predictions change if the number line segment selected for the random walk activity were longer, say 12 units on a side instead of 10?

Keep going. Have the students investigate a random walk on the computer. For this, the students need a watch with a second hand or a stopwatch, Logo software, and a computer.

Explain that RANDOM 20 outputs a random number 0 through 19. Have the students enter the following command several times and observe the turtle's behavior:

    FD RANDOM 20 RT RANDOM 360

Have them estimate how long it will take the turtle to walk off any edge of the screen if they keep repeating those commands. Check their estimates by typing the following command after clearing the screen:

    REPEAT 10000 [FD RANDOM 20 RT RANDOM 360]

One member of a pair of students should time (in seconds) how long it takes the turtle to walk off the edge of the screen. The other student should watch the screen to let the timer know when this happens by quietly saying "off." The pair should keep a record of the seconds for each of twenty walks.

Society's increasing use of technology requires that students learn...to communicate with computers.... (NCTM 1989a, p. 78)

Collect and graph the class data and discuss how each pair's results compare to the class results.

As a challenge, ask the students to estimate how long it will take if the following command is given:

REPEAT 10000 [FD RANDOM 10 RT RANDOM 360]

Have them check their estimate with the turtle. What will happen if other numbers are used? Will the turtle always walk off an edge eventually?

A RANDOM WALK

1. To determine a walk, chose any six contiguous numbers in a line or column on the Random Number Table. These six numbers give the six steps of the walk.

2. On the number line, begin at O. Move the number of units specified for each step. If the number is odd, move left. If the number is even, move right.

3. Take six steps and record where you land in the table below.

4. For the next walk, choose six numbers in any row or column.

5. Take ten walks, each of six steps.

RANDOM NUMBER TABLE

3	1	1	6	3	3	4	2	6	6	5	4
6	4	3	5	6	1	5	4	4	2	4	3
5	6	1	5	4	1	3	2	2	6	1	1
1	5	6	2	2	1	4	4	1	5	3	2
5	3	6	1	2	5	1	2	6	3	3	1
5	2	1	6	5	1	4	2	3	1	5	3
2	3	5	6	2	4	4	2	5	2	3	2
4	6	4	1	6	4	6	4	4	4	3	6
5	4	4	6	4	2	4	1	2	5	2	1
5	1	6	4	4	3	1	6	5	2	3	1
3	3	6	1	1	2	6	2	1	4	4	3
5	2	5	5	1	1	5	6	3	4	4	6

Walk one: show your steps.

Left off | | | | | | | | | | | | | | | | | | | | | Right off

L10 L9 L8 L7 L6 L5 L4 L3 L2 L1 O R1 R2 R3 R4 R5 R6 R7 R8 R9 R10

Use this number line for the rest of your walks. If you want to show all steps, draw your own number line.

Left off | | | | | | | | | | | | | | | | | | | | | Right off

L10 L9 L8 L7 L6 L5 L4 L3 L2 L1 O R1 R2 R3 R4 R5 R6 R7 R8 R9 R10

Record where you landed on each of the ten walks.

Left off	L10	L9	L8	L7	L6	L5	L4	L3	L2	L1	O	R1	R2	R3	R4	R5	R6	R7	R8	R9	R10	Right off

GEOMETRY AND SPATIAL SENSE

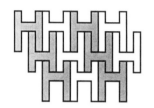

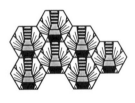

Students in grade 5 have an interest in the way things fit together. Activities selected for fifth graders should suggest ways of linking mathematics with other subjects and ways of linking branches of mathematics together. The study of tessellations is particularly rich in applications to other fields, for example, to the study of wallpaper designs, fabric prints, and the art of graphic artists such as M. C. Escher. The use of activity centers or other small-group work encourages the growth of language—the language of mathematics as well as language about mathematics.

Many students at this grade level are still dependent on concrete referents; therefore, activities presented here depend heavily on the use of materials. Manipulatives support and enrich the student's conceptual growth and are especially important for the development of geometric and spatial sense.

Research strongly suggests that continued experience with two- and three-dimensional figures throughout the grades builds a firm foundation for the more formal geometry of secondary school. Unless students have these rich experiences, more advanced geometric concepts will be beyond their reach.

Students' understanding of the angle properties of polygons and the concept of area can be enhanced through explorations of tessellations with regular polygons. (NCTM 1989a, p. 115)

TILING WITH PLANE FIGURES

Get ready. The purpose of this activity is to have students discover geometric figures that tile a plane.

Builders make walls by fitting together large numbers of identical geometric solids. Many driveways and walks are paved with interlocking bricks of various sizes and shapes. Covering a flat surface by using one or more geometric figures should lead to investigating tiling patterns.

A tessellation is a design that covers a flat surface without leaving gaps and without overlapping. Building a tiling pattern may involve slides, flips, or turns and the physical and mental manipulation of geometric figures, which are important ingredients of spatial sense. Since a plane extends forever in all directions, a tessellation need not fit the borders of the page exactly. However, it should be apparent that the pattern can be extended indefinitely in all directions.

The materials needed are tagboard, tape, rulers, scissors, construction paper, pattern blocks, dot paper, counters (circular), and transparencies of dot paper that show tessellations of triangles and of other figures on dot paper. A blackline master for two types of dot paper can be found on page 32.

A tiling pattern is also called a tessellation.

Get going. Have the students use rulers to draw carefully on tagboard a triangle about the size of a playing card. Encourage each member of the class to make a different triangle. Have them cut out their triangle to use as a template to make about twenty more copies.

Have the students use only the copies of their own triangle to tessellate a portion of their desk top.

As they look at one another's work, ask questions that focus on their tessellations:

Could you all tile a portion of your desk with your triangles?

How big an area do you think you could cover if eighty more copies of your triangle were available?

How many copies of your triangle do you think it would take to cover the classroom floor?

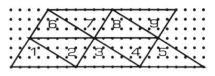

Make a transparency of the illustrated tessellation. From colored acetate or paper, cut a triangle the same size as triangle 1. Place this triangle on top of triangle 1. Tell the class you want them to help you move the triangle around on the transparency *without picking it up*. Call individuals to the overhead projector and ask them to make and describe the following moves:

> position 1 to position 3 [slide]
>
> position 1 to position 2 [turn]
>
> position 1 to position 8 [slide]

Extend the discussion:

If a triangle is moved from position 1 to another position by a slide, what are the possible positions?

What positions can a triangle occupy after a slide and a turn?

How can a triangle be moved from position 1 to position 9? Is there another way? [slide and turn]

The above discussion illustrates slides and turns only. Flips can be demonstrated by allowing the students to pick up the triangle.

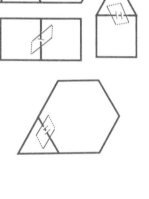

Put the students in small groups. Have them tape two pattern blocks together to make a new figure. Encourage the class to make a variety. Have each group select one of the taped figures and make several identical figures. Ask the students to use their constructed figures to tile a portion of their desk top.

Is there a pattern? Can it be extended?

Did some figures tessellate more easily than others? Why?

Identify examples of slides, flips, or turns.

Have the students look for tessellations in the real world, such as rectangular bricks in the walls of houses. Encourage them to draw some of the interesting ones they find to share with the class.

Keep going. Display the illustrated figures on the overhead projector. Have the students copy one of the figures onto square dot paper, cut out six to eight copies, and test the figure to see if it tessellates. [Each one will.] Have the students draw their own figures and test them to see if they will tessellate. Collect samples of other figures that tessellate and figures that do not. Display the collections on the bulletin board.

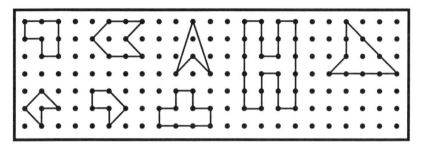

SIMILAR FIGURES

Get ready. The purpose of this activity is to give children experience in identifying and drawing similar figures. Materials needed are cubes and pattern blocks.

Get going. Ask the students to use the word *similar* in a sentence.

Explain to the students that the word *similar* belongs to everyday language and has been adopted by mathematicians and given a highly specialized meaning. These uses exist side by side; we must learn to use the term accurately in different contexts.

Put the students in small groups and ask them to make different-sized squares by using squares from a set of pattern blocks.

How many squares are needed? Can you build a square with twenty-seven square pattern blocks?

What is the smallest square you can make? What is the next largest? The next?

Similarity can also be related to such real-world contexts as photographs, models, projections of pictures, and photocopy machines. (NCTM 1989a, p. 114)

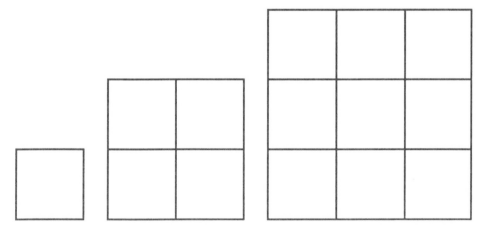

Ask the students to look at the squares that have been made and to compare the lengths of their sides and their areas. [These squares are all similar.]

Is it possible to make squares that are not similar? What about triangles? If a square has sides twice as long as those of another square, is its area twice as much? What about its perimeter?

Students should explore the relationships among the lengths, areas, and volumes of similar solids. (NCTM 1989a, p. 114)

Using the pattern block triangles, repeat the previous activity. Tell the children to record the number of blocks in each figure.

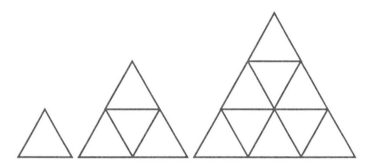

Repeat the activity using the rhombus in the pattern block set. Again, the figures are similar.

Ask the students if they see a pattern in the number of blocks needed to make successive similar figures for squares, triangles, and rhombuses. Students may recognize these as the "square numbers": 1, 4, 9, 16.

Keep going. To extend the activity, use cubes to explore similarities in three dimensions.

How many cubes do you think it will take to make a cube twice as high? Try it and see! Three times as high?

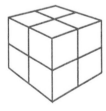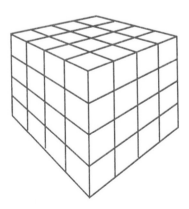

To double each dimension requires 8 times as many cubes.

LOGO AND SIMILAR FIGURES

Get ready. The purpose of this activity is to have students explore the properties of similar figures by using the geometric turtle graphics of Logo.

The materials required are paper, pencils, rulers, and computers with Logo.

Get going. Logo activities can help students build on their intuitions to develop more explicit mathematical ideas of geometric figures. For example, to develop a procedure for outlining a figure, children must connect the visual characteristics of a figure, the turtle movements, and the mathematical properties of the figure.

If computers are not available, Logo activities can be mirrored by having the children "walk out" the instructions using one "heel-to-toe" to be equivalent to ten "turtle steps."

In Logo, an on-screen "turtle" responds to instructions to draw geometric figures.
FORWARD 50 (or FD 50)
instructs the turtle to move forward 50 "turtle steps" in whatever direction it is pointing. Other commands include the following:
RIGHT 90 (RT 90): *Rotate 90 degrees to the right.*
LEFT 90 (LT 90): *Rotate 90 degrees to the left.*
PENUP (PU): *Put the pen up, so that a path is not drawn.*
PENDOWN (PD): *Put the pen down, so that a path is drawn.*
HT: *Hide the turtle.*
ST: *Show the turtle.*
Commands to clear the screen differ; try CS, DRAW, *or* CG.

Write the instructions below on an overhead transparency or on the chalkboard. The first instruction, TO R1, names the program that draws a rectangle whose name is R1. Have the children walk out each procedure to insure that it does indeed give a rectangle.

TO R1	TO R2	TO R3
FD 30	FD 60	FD 15
RT 90	LT 90	RT 90
FD 50	FD 100	FD 25
RT 90	LT 90	RT 90
FD 30	FD 60	FD 15
RT 90	LT 90	RT 90
FD 50	FD 100	FD 25
END	END	END

Students should also draw the figure on dot or graph paper.

If a computer is available, run the first program. Ask the students to read the programs for R2 and R3 and predict how the rectangles will be different.

Every classroom will have at least one computer available at all times for demonstrations and student use. (NCTM 1989a, p. 68)

Compare these three procedures for drawing rectangles.

Ask the students to compare how the rectangles are alike and how they are different:

How are the commands for the three rectangles the same? [The turn commands specify right-angle turns.]

How are they different? [The forward commands are different.]

How are the lengths of the sides of R1 and R2 related? [The ratio of the lengths of the corresponding sides is 1:2.] *Of R1 and R3?* [The ratio of the lengths of the corresponding sides is 2:1.] *Of R2 and R3?* [The ratio of the lengths of the corresponding sides is 4:1.]

What does it mean for two figures to be similar?

Keep going. Have each student draw a rectangle and write the Logo program to generate it. Suggest that students compare their programs and find all the rectangles created by their classmates that are similar to their own.

Are all rectangles similar? Why not?

Exercises that ask children to visualize, draw, and compare shapes in various positions will help develop their spatial sense. (NCTM 1989a, p. 48)

DRAWING AND BUILDING SOLIDS MADE OF CUBES

Get ready. The purpose of this activity is to have children investigate solids made with cubes and draw the solids on triangle (isometric) dot paper.

The materials needed for this activity are triangle dot paper, pencils, and cubes. A sample of triangle dot paper can be found on page 32.

◆　　◆　　◆　　◆　　◆　　◆　　◆　　◆

Get going. A student's ability to think, reason, and solve problems is greatly enhanced by the use of manipulatives. Drawing geometric solids is a desirable skill. This activity is one of the many steps in helping students acquire this skill.

The task of making a two-dimensional drawing of a three-dimensional object can be difficult. Triangle dot paper makes drawing three-dimensional solids easier.

Triangle dot paper is made up of dots at the vertices of equilateral triangles. Note that one edge of the triangle is vertical. We usually use the triangle dot paper in this position. However, if the triangle dot paper is rotated through 90°, one edge of the triangle is now horizontal, and a different view of the figure is obtained. Usually the first orientation is easier to use for drawing objects.

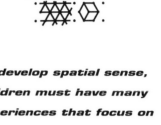

Give each student several pieces of triangle dot paper. Make and display a transparency of the figures below. Have the students copy each drawing onto triangle dot paper and use cubes to make models of each represented solid.

To develop spatial sense, children must have many experiences that focus on geometric relationships; the direction, orientation, and perspectives of objects in space.... (NCTM 1989a, p. 49)

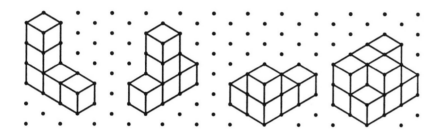

Make and display a transparency of the figures below. Have the students copy each solid shown onto triangle dot paper and draw lines to show the individual cubes. Have the students use cubes to make solids like the ones they have drawn.

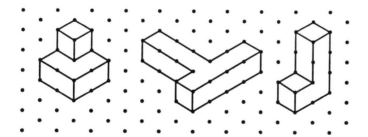

Ask the students to place two cubes face-to-face in front of them and to draw a picture of the two cubes on triangle dot paper. Ask them to form a solid with three cubes joined face-to-face and draw it on triangle dot paper.

Keep going. Have the students put three or four cubes together to make a solid and draw two different views of the solid on triangle dot paper.

Have the students draw pictures of different solids on their triangle dot paper. Can each figure be constructed? Challenge the students to draw a figure that cannot be constructed (see illustration at the right).

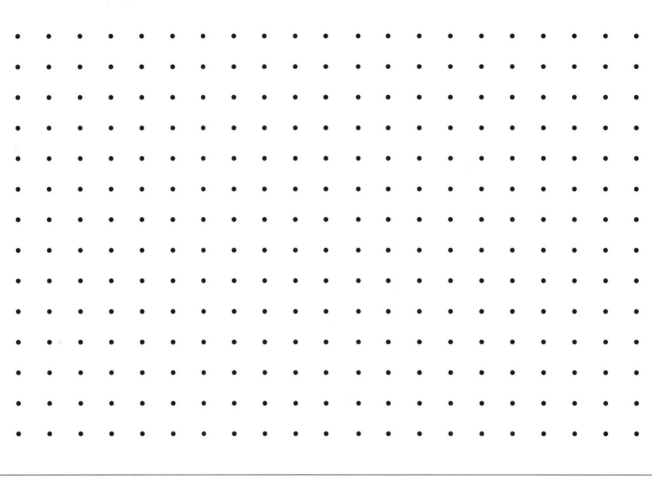